Animals and Tools

Matt Reher Kristina Rupp

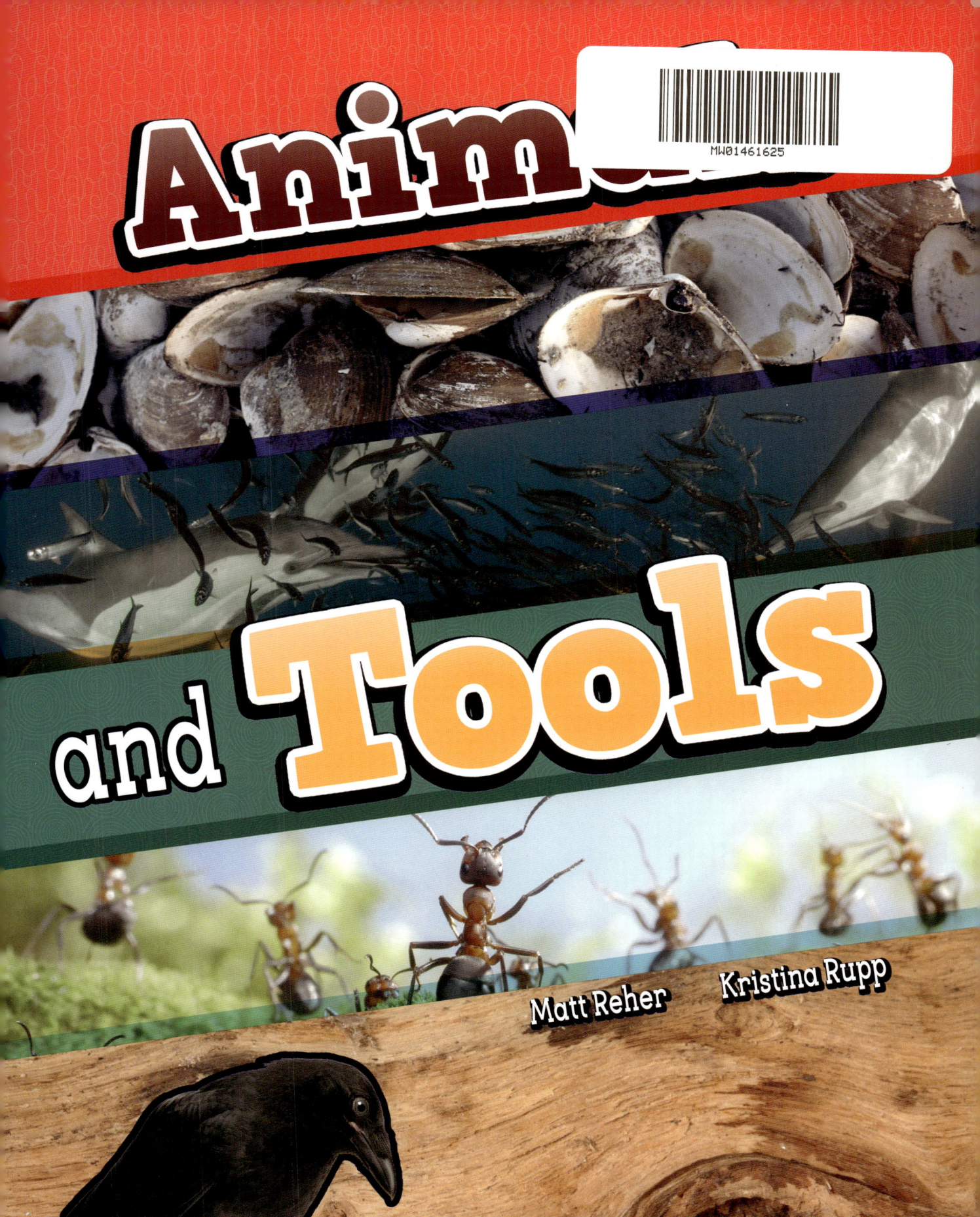

What's Inside?

- **4** Lots of Tools
- **6** Chimps
- **8** Dolphins
- **10** Elephants
- **12** Otters
- **14** Ants
- **16** Birds
- **24** Word Tools

pg. 14

pg. 20

pg. 12

Lots of Tools

When you think of tools, do you think of tools like these? These are all tools.

But, so are all of these.

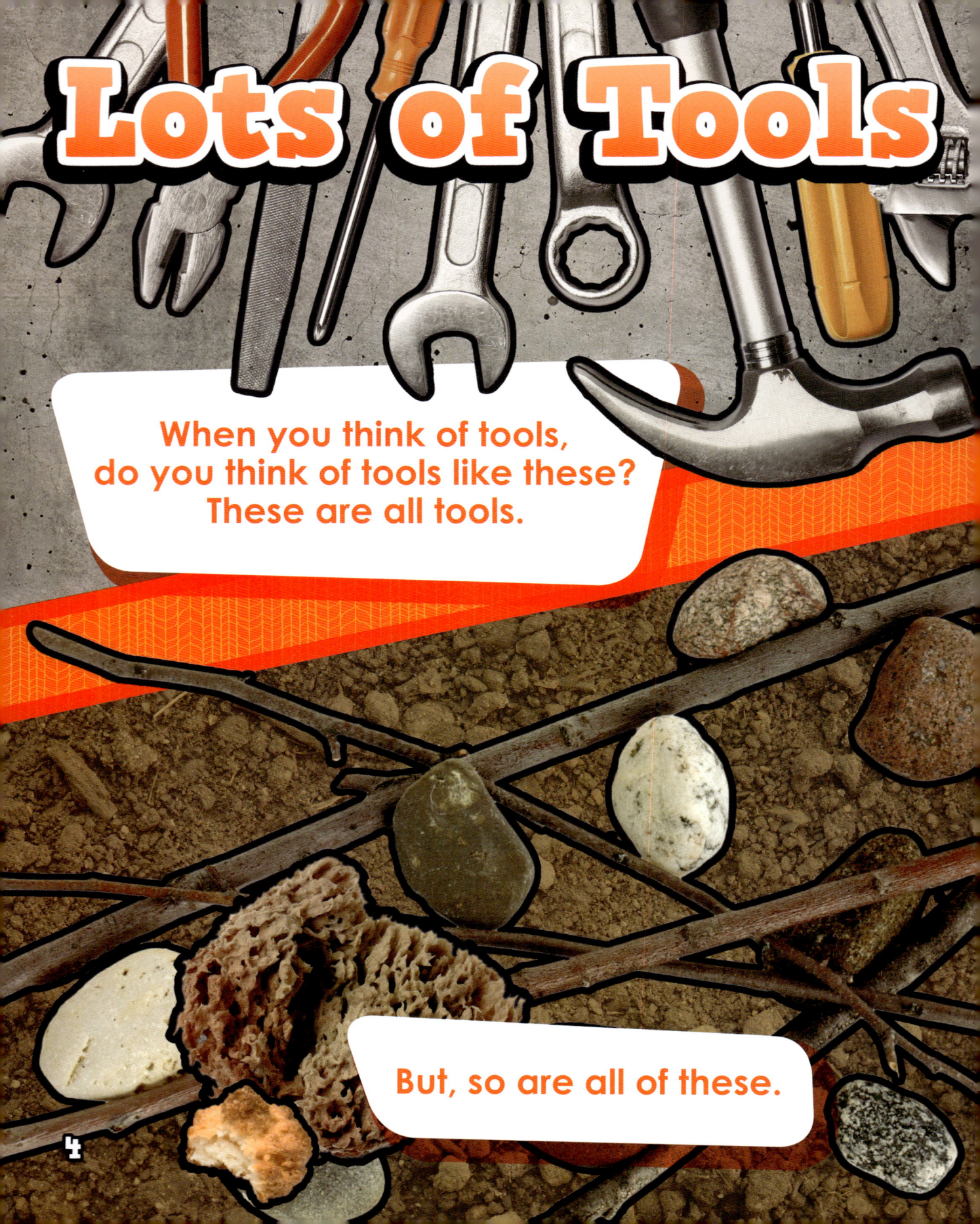

We have hands. Our hands can do lots of things. But tools let us do things that our hands can't do, like make homes and knit clothes.

Some animals use tools, too. They use tools to get and eat food. They get tools from where they live.

Then she puts the tall, thin stick into the hill. When she takes the stick out, there are lots of bugs on it. She doesn't kill the bugs. She eats them live! When she has had her fill of bugs, she goes.

all

get

Dolphins

Dolphins eat fish. The fish want to live. So, the fish go down into the wet sand. Now how will the dolphins get the fish? A net?

No. Dolphins don't get a net. They get this. It looks like a plant, but it's an animal. We call it a sponge. The dolphin gets a sponge. She sets it on her snout.

The sponge is like a pillow.

8

black Otters

Otters love to snack on clams. Clams are inside shells. So, how do the otters get the clams?

Wow, Jack! Where did you track down so many clams?

sea otter

ant

Ants

There are many ant families. Some eat plants. Ants don't want ants that aren't in their family to get the plants. So, how do they stop them?

Drop it! We want your food!

Shrikes

I bet I'd be top bird with big hands.

This bird wants to eat some bits of this bug, not all of it. She doesn't have hands to take the bits she wants. How will she eat it?

She hops up on a plant. The plant has thorns. She sets the bug on a thorn. Now she can eat the bits of the bug that she wants to eat.

I do this to mice, small birds, and lizards, too.

Tools are all around us. I'll bet you didn't think that so many animals could use so many tools.